# Harvesttime

# Apples

## By Inez Snyder

**Welcome Books™**

SCHOLASTIC INC.

New York  Toronto  London  Auckland  Sydney
Mexico City  New Delhi  Hong Kong  Buenos Aires

Contributing Editors: Jennifer Silate and Shira Laskin
Book Design: Erica Clendening

ISBN 0-516-25544-4

# Contents

Apples grow from **seeds**.

Apple seeds grow into trees.

Apple trees can grow
very tall.

Some apples turn red when they are ready to be **harvested**.

Most apples are ready to be picked in the **fall**.

Apple pickers **climb** ladders to reach the apples.

11

Apple pickers pick the apples carefully.

They do not want to **bruise** the apples.

13

After the apples are picked,
they are put on a truck.

15

The truck will take the apples to a **warehouse**.

At the warehouse, people pack the apples in boxes.

The boxes of apples are sent to stores.

People can buy apples at the stores.

RED DELICIOUS
$1.19 LB

19

Many people like to eat apples.

# New Words

bruise (**brooz**) to make a dark mark on
something by dropping or hitting it

climb (**klime**) to move up something
using your hands and feet

fall (**fawl**) the season between summer
and winter

harvested (**hahr**-vuhst-uhd) picked
or gathered

seeds (**seedz**) the parts of plants that
can grow in soil and make new plants

warehouse (**wair**-hous) a large building
used for storing goods

# To Find Out More

## Books

*How Do Apples Grow?*
by Betsy C. Maestro
HarperCollins Children's Books

*Picking Apples and Pumpkins*
by Amy Hutchings
Scholastic Inc.

## Web Site

**Just for Kids**
http://www.bestapples.com/kids/
Learn about apples, what animals eat them, and play fun games on this Web site.

# Index

**About the Author**

Inez Snyder has written several books to help children learn to read. She also enjoys cooking for her family.

**Reading Consultants**

Kris Flynn, Coordinator, Small School District Literacy, The San Diego County Office of Education

Shelly Forys, Certified Reading Recovery Specialist, W.J. Zahnow Elementary School, Waterloo, IL

Paulette Mansell, Certified Reading Recovery Specialist, and Early Literacy Consultant, TX